OKEHAM of Yesteryear

Mike and Hilary Wreford

OBELISK PUBLICATIONS

Also by the Authors

Okehampton Collection
Okehampton Collection II
Okehampton Collection III
Okehampton People

Other Titles in this Series

Ashburton of Yesteryear, *John Germon and Pete Webb*
The Teign Valley of Yesteryear, Parts I and II, *Chips Barber*
Brixham of Yesteryear, Parts I, II and III, *Chips Barber*
Pinhoe of Yesteryear, Parts I and II, *Chips Barber*
Princetown of Yesteryear, Parts I and II, *Chips Barber*
Kingsteignton of Yesteryear, *Richard Harris*
Heavitree of Yesteryear, *Chips Barber*
Kenton and Starcross of Yesteryear, *Eric Vaughan*
Ide of Yesteryear, *Mavis Piller*
Exmouth Century, Parts One and Two, *George Pridmore*

We have over 160 Devon titles; for a full list please send an SAE to Obelisk Publications, 2 Church Hill, Pinhoe, Exeter EX4 9ER

Acknowledgements

Special thanks to Barrie Hall of Okehampton for permission to use his pictures. Also thanks to Joan Pauley, Yvonne Rendle, Jean Williams, Colin Lennox-Jones, Gillian Partridge, Jeffe Cunliffe, Pam Norris, Helen Cann and Raymond Vallance and to all those who gave up their valuable time for interviews and anecdotes of past times.
The Town Crest is reproduced by kind permission of Okehampton Town Council.

First published in 2000 by
Obelisk Publications, 2 Church Hill, Pinhoe, Exeter, Devon
Designed and Typeset by Sally Barber
Printed in Great Britain

OKEHAMPTON

of Yesteryear

As the new Millennium approaches we thought that it was an opportune time to take a look back at Okehampton over the last hundred years or so, this being about the limit of photographic coverage. Turning back the clock can be a fascinating business – forgotten places and faces returning almost ghost-like from the past. One's memory is a powerful thing and we are sure that this book will trigger many memories from Okehampton's past.

For example, it is not generally known that Fore Street had a "Middle Row" of properties which extended from St James Chapel to a point close to the Plume of Feathers. The 'other' street was Back Street, this providing a narrow entrance between the church and what is now Angus McPhie's. The Guildhall was also at the end of this "Middle Row" and it is a pity that this run of buildings was demolished.

But this is what this book is all about. Had all the streets and the buildings in them stayed the same then this collection of pictures, and the memories which accompany them, would have been almost meaningless. Okehampton is no different to any town but for us it is "home" and we hope you will derive immense pleasure, as we have done, from this photographic look-back at an "Okehampton of Yesteryear". To this end we have devoted much time and energy.

As is always the case, we have done our best to identify people in pictures, but sometimes this has proved difficult or impossible. We apologise for any errors or omissions in this respect.

Celebrations were held in the Castle in July 1973 to mark the 350th anniversary of the granting of the Charter by King James I to Okehampton in 1623. The maypole dancing was held in Okehampton's Old Park as it preceded the pageant at the Castle.

Amongst the children pictured are Katherine Chowings, Mary Stevens, Susie Bessell, Angela Brockman, Johnny Harding, Tony Gilbert, David Hutchinson, Steve Gilbert, Stewart MacCullock, Susie Welham, Mark Hawkins, Ian Kiely and Roger Cann.

Everyone in the town seemed to support and enjoy this unique event and it lasted from 14 July to 29 July. It started with a civic procession from Market Street to Simmons Park and the whole fortnight was packed with events, including the sports week. A notable touch was that the ancient Curfew was rung at 7 a.m. and 8 p.m. daily from the tower of St James' Church.

The picture below (opposite) is of Okehampton Borough Council and officers in the Town Hall at a time when local government reorganisation was looming. However, they were determined at this time to celebrate the 1623 Charter. They were all personally involved and sportingly played their part in the historical pageant under the guidance of R. L. Taverner and Terry Bennett. There was also the redevelopment of the Market Hall and the Turret Room, which was opened in that period to celebrate the event. The architect of this improvement was Peter Woodgate, whose work has so often benefited the town in great style.

Back row: Ron Taylor, C. E. W. (Clem) White, W. J. Passmore (Mayor), Reg Horne, Jimmy Crocker. Middle row: Dick Elliott, Peter Woodgate, Derek Allin, Harry Matthews, Terry Bennett (Borough Surveyor), Jeffe Cunliffe. Front row: Bill Letchford, Dr C. G. Jones, Arthur Dear (Town Clerk), Margaret Nash, Polly White, Joan Pauley.

Pictured above are members of the Red Cross in 1960. They had regular weekly training sessions at the top room in the Pretoria Hotel. This celebratory "get together" was to welcome the Red Cross County Commander, Sir Trefry Thompson. Their medical adviser was the popular Okehampton GP Jean Shields and that popularity can be judged by the considerable strength of the Red Cross at the time.

Back row: Julia Rudd, Heather Mallett, Sheila Rutley, Denelene Coles, Brenda Meardon, Kay Weeks, Sally Brock, Pauline Green, Marion Thomas, Josephine Cox, (?), Dawn Preece, Carol Aggett, Miriam Glover. Amongst the third row are: Sheila Squires, Gwen Hodge, (?), Mrs Hannaford, (?), (?), Joan Pauley, Mrs Tancock, Mrs Pelly, Margaret Cook, (?), Margaret Reddaway, (?), Lil Hosgood, Ivy Aggett, (?), Frances Wonnacott, Mrs Winterburn, Mina Darch. Second row: Polly Finch, Doris Cawse, Mrs N. Bendyshe, Sister Hawkins, Miss Kingsford Lethbridge, Sir Trefry Thompson, Dr Jean Shields, Polly White, Ivy Carew. Front row: Janet Nicholls, Sonia Guest, Brenda Barnes (behind), Carol Hubber, Carol Hawkins, Sandra Devonald, Denise Scantlebury, Jennifer Allin, Valerie Godfrey, Megan Devonald, Sally Connor, Susan Cox (behind), Muriel Westlake, Wendy Cook.

The staff of the North Street Primary School were keen to encourage young children to perform on stage at an early age, to give them confidence. This cast of eight-year-olds showed no sign of nerves as they performed Enid Blyton's story "Crying for the Moon" produced by their teacher, Mrs E. G. Yeo, on 22 June 1950. It was a team effort with the costumes made by parents and teachers, who also did much more besides.

Back row: Terry Acton, Olive Dowden, Maureen Bradbury, Peter Henwood, Yvonne Bray, Audrey Metherell, Ryan Roberts. Front row: Sheila Welham, Tricia Fry, Colin Rudd, Marcia Yeo, Rosalind Talbot, Joyce Rice, Michael King.

In the early 1950s the Okehampton Show was used as a location for the feature film *Cast a Dark Shadow*. There was filming throughout show day, with the exhibitors being paid extra to leave their stands in place until the Sunday for additional scenes. Many locals were used as extras, and were paid 10s 6d (52½p) per day.

There was great excitement with the presence of stars such as Patrick Holt, Elizabeth Sellars and Lana Morris, and many Okehampton people were in the audience when the film was later shown at the Carlton Cinema.

The children of the Okehampton Primary School always enjoyed their Christmas gift visits to the Okehampton Castle Hospital. This pictured visit, however, was at the time of the 1969 Harvest Festival and young Louise Hellyer is handing her present personally to Matron Talbot. The presents were provided by parents, teachers and children, who were able to share in the joy with the patients and nurses. The staff, left to right, are Lil Hosgood, Grace Gay, Louise King, Margaret Shepherd and Ivy Down.

No history of the last 100 years would be complete without mention of the sterling work of the Home Guard. The photograph below shows the Okehampton/Folly Gate section at Okehampton Aerodrome. All Home Guard personnel, of course, had their normal essential work to follow during the War, devoting almost all of their spare time to guarding the country. This group features, in true "Dad's Army" tradition, bank official and Second Lieutenant Rex Lennox-Jones (middle centre) with Sergeants George Whieldon and Lesley Eyke on the flanks. Also included are Roy Edmonds, Sidney Stanbury, Percy (Rocky) Cleave, Stanley Stanbury, Jimmy Reddaway (Cpl), Frank Yeo (Cpl), Henry Hooper and Vince Rees.

Winston Churchill was proud of the Home Guard, who were originally named the LDV (Local Defence Volunteers), with much of their training in the early days being done with broomsticks and pikes, rifles being in short supply.

It is 1947 and the children of North Street Primary School are smiling. The evacuees have returned to the big cities and class sizes have, as a result, reduced. Some of the children were seeing more of their fathers, who had now returned from all parts of the globe. Back row: Pam Ware, Marian Williams, Mary Squires, Maribel Bond, (?), Muriel Evans, Hazel Metherell, Jean Wright, Jacky Cooper. Third row: Michael Smale, Kathleen Crocker, Eunice Stone, Madeline Pedrick, Ann Watkins, Vivienne Cummings, Margaret Allen-Price, Pam Voaden, Jennifer Kelland, Eric King. Second row: Keith Lower, Bill Stanley, Michael Kelly, Tony Perry, George Maddaford, Paul Hendry, Michael Smith, Michael Hedden. Front row: John Hearn, Billy Walters, John Bolt, Derek Welham, Jimmy Westlake, Brian Short.

Below we see the Inter House competition on sports day. In this mid-1950s shot there were some outstanding athletes, who carried their all-round sports ability into adult life and represented the town in various team sports. Back row: Brian Hodgetts, David Bubear, Elizabeth Carter, Stephen Bickle, Jean Read, Ronald Collins, David Hedderley, Christopher Walker, Kenneth Kingsley-Williams, Pat Sandercock, Edward King, Janet Ware, Bronwen Lobb, Raymond Rattenbury. Middle row: Jenny Dennis, Linda Rudd, Joyce Rice, Maureen Fanning, Celia Doidge, Bob Gee, Michael Turner, Gordon King, Malcolm (?), Michael Bevan, Jeanette Hatten, Jean Eggleton, Christine Brown, Marion D(?). Front row: Graham Hosgood, David Voaden, Jennifer Bassett, Ann Stone, Adrian Barnard, Sally Pedrick, John Day, Ann Roberts, Eugene Southcott, Pat Harding, Judy Feaver, Pat Goodanew, Mary Connor.

Here we have Okehampton Old Time Dancing Club with its large membership at the 1950s Annual Charity Ball at the Market Hall, and many of the faces will be instantly recognised. This was a thriving club for many years, with weekly dancing at the secondary modern school in Exeter Road, now the police station. This club continued for many years, with the members always immaculately dressed and not a "Rock and Roller" in sight. Miss Greep was an excellent instructor, no doubt calling on all her schoolteaching skills for these mature students.

April 1983 was the date of retirement for long-serving Town Clerk Arthur Dear and the official presentation on behalf of the Council was made by Polly White. David Voaden, his successor as Clerk, is shown on Mrs White's right. Pictured left to right are: Harry Matthews, Ron Taylor, Pauline Fletcher, David Voaden, Vic Savage, Polly White, Joan Pauley, Mary Vick, Bill Letchford, Arthur Dear, Brenda Savage, Walter Passmore, Jeffe Cunliffe, Ray Vallance, Peter Woodgate and Janet Voaden.

FULFORD

The torrential rain of 19/20 August 1950 caused the town's rivers to rise to dangerous levels, the worst affected area being West Bridge, and the top two pictures opposite illustrate the problem. The Okehampton Castle Laundry at Castleford was badly hit. Something had to be done and schemes were already in hand, not only to alleviate the flooding but also to improve the A30 road to Cornwall. There have also been some other changes, with the G. U. Fulford Ltd building being demolished and the old St John's Church being replaced by the Church Hall.

The third picture shows a part of Okehampton that has completely changed in more recent years. The Mill Road entrance was a danger to motor vehicles and pedestrians alike. The workshop on the left, used by Freddie Barnicoat, was demolished, along with the row of cottages on the right, whose occupants included chimney sweeps Harris and Sid Voysey. The old Lillicraps and the East Street Methodist Church went as well and we now have the more modern and useful dwellings of today, providing essential accommodation, near the town centre.

The Mayor's Parade of 1957 is seen here, marching along Vicarage Road. It is interesting to note how narrow the road was, and the absence of any housing development. In the front it is easy to identify the more senior members of the Red Cross as follows: Janie Mortimer, Doris Cawse, Josey Marles (senior cadet), Joan Mason (in the middle), Polly Finch, Pauline Day (senior cadet), Jean Marles (senior cadet), Mrs Winterburn and Mrs Pelley.

The American Army were popular visitors to Okehampton during the War and here they are pictured at the Church Parade in May 1944. They were based at the Showfield Camp during their "rehearsals" for D-Day, from which, sadly, some were not to return. They soon integrated into the local community and were popular with the children as they arranged parties for them. During the War years the Mayor was George Gratton, with long-serving Town Clerk J. J. Newcombe on his left. Home Guard Captain and local businessman George Whieldon is on the right with the baton. The macebearers are Jimmy Johns and Joe Yelland. This photograph was supplied by an American officer with some fond memories of Okehampton, who returned many years later.

The Drill Hall is used by many organisations for charitable and other purposes. It has also been the venue for many excellent social events and the Conservative Club has continued this fine tradition since taking the premises in 1969. Here, on 25 November 1974, the club organised "A Cockney Evening in Edwardian Style". Pictured left to right: Derek Adams, Reg Cullington, Kirby Tippett, Diana Stanus, Betty Ashcroft, Grace Easterbrook, Dorothy Martin, Millie Newcombe (President), Vera Hodgkinson.

The Drill Hall had been opened on 1 July 1914 for military and social purposes of the local Company of the 6th Devon Regiment and had served the country through two world wars.

The Annual Okehampton Conservative Club Dinner/Dance on 9 October 1971 was, as usual, well attended during the presidency of Brenda Savage. Brenda and husband Vic both went on to become Mayors of Okehampton – a popular husband-and-wife team. Left to right: Vic Savage, Nina Talbot, Cecil Cole, Mavis Cornish, Brenda Savage, Derek Adams, John Talbot, Millie Newcombe, John Yelland, Fred Reynolds, Susan Reynolds, Gordon Wilson, Peggy Wilson.

Simmons Park was always a popular place for group photographs and this 1920s Brownie pack was no exception, pictured here having a picnic. All aged between eight and eleven years, these girls went on to become Girl Guides. As this was in the formative days of the Brownies, very few had uniforms, although Crissie Stoneman seems to be wearing a new Brownie outfit. Nurse Grimaldi was the old-fashioned type of District Nurse in Okehampton for many years and had probably helped bring many of these young ladies into the world. Back row: Janie Marles, Nurse Grimaldi, (?). Third row: Crissie Stoneman (Lobb), Lucy Seymour, Lilian Haines, Winnie Chudley, Doris Virgin (Pedrick), Hilda Drew. Second row: Cissie Webber, Dorothy Youlden, Gertie Hunkin, Coey Cornish, Meggie Hodge, Lilian Collacott, Kath Cox (Ware). Front row: Joan Webber (Collacott), Betty Martin.

In 1970 three Okehampton Girl Guides, Diane Rendle, Hazel Sampson and Angela Lee, assembled in the Congregational Schoolroom in North Street to be presented with well-deserved Queen's Guide Awards. This building is now Okehampton Library. Left to right: Marion Cosway, (?), Jane Chammings, Betty Letchford, Tonya Banks, Diane Rendle, the District Commissioner, Marion Rendle, Carol Smallacombe, Sue Finch, Linda Finch, Hazel Sampson, Angela Lee, Janet Harris, Margaret Savage, Jill Kelly (almost hidden), Alison Hawken, Vanessa Kinsey, Frances Blatchford.

The White Hart Hotel has held many celebratory banquets for Members of Parliament, such as Thomas Tyrwhitt, Admiral Rodney, John Charles Spencer, George Littleton and three members of the Pitt Family, including the great Earl of Chatham. This 1959 event celebrated the election of the popular Conservative MP Percy Browne, a highly respected local farmer and road haulier. With an outstanding and lively personality, he was commissioned in the Royal Dragoons during the War, serving in North Africa, Sicily and North West Europe. He also rode in the 1953 Grand National and surely not many MPs can claim that distinction. Sadly ill-health caused him to retire from politics in 1964 and a potentially brilliant parliamentary career was curtailed. Featured at the top table are, left to right: Colonel H. C. Kingsford-Lethbridge, Mrs Meg Daniel, Mr Percy

Browne MP, Lt Col D. F. Brown TD, Captain William Daniel, Mrs Jennifer Browne, Mr John Yelland. This was when Okehampton was in the Torrington constituency and Percy defeated the strong Liberal Candidate, Mark Bonham-Carter. The votes were cast as follows: Browne, P. B. (Con) (Elected) 17,283; Carter, M. R. Bonham (Lib) 15,018; Dobson, R. F. H. (Lab) 5,633; Conservative majority 2,265. Percy's successor was the equally popular Peter Mills, later Sir Peter, who commanded great support from all parties and represented the constituency for many years.

The *Okehampton Times* provided the history of the next photograph (opposite, bottom) and a revelation to those who listened to the 21-gun Royal Salute in Okehampton in celebration of the Coronation in 1953. *"The truth, reflected in this picture, is that there was no 21-gun salute in Okehampton on the occasion of the Coronation – whatever you might have thought you heard. The Mayor, Dr C. G. Jones, seen in the picture with two of his children, confronted a crisis. The people of Okehampton felt there should be a 21-gun salute for the Coronation. The military up at the camp said they could not do it. So he turned to Meldon Quarry, and in particular, Mr Lyndon Weaver, manager of the quarry, on the extreme right of the picture. 'Could you', he asked Mr Weaver, 'produce a sound just like a 21-gun salute with explosives from your quarry?' After thought and consultation, the answer was 'Yes' and it was all set up on a field above the town, where this photograph was taken on Coronation Day 1953. Skilled men from the quarry set off a series of 4-ounce charges on the field which were timed by listening to radio commentaries to coincide exactly with the salute in London."* The others pictured, left to right, are blastmen Fred Parish, Jack Fellow and Nim Palmer, followed by Dr William Dearman, assistant manager at the quarry.

It's tea and cakes for the ladies of the Okehampton Congregational Church in North Street in 1947 – a church with a fine tradition, which did much for so many generations, and it was a sad day when it closed its doors on 10 March 1974. The church had been built in 1800, and rebuilt in 1820. It could seat 320 and often had a full congregation. It was part and parcel of Okehampton life. The Congregationalists of the early part of this century could be a very formidable body. The men would dress in their sober Sunday best and gather for innocent recreation as was appropriate to the Sabbath at the time. It was a federation called PSA and it stood for "Pleasant Sunday Afternoon". It seems that women were excluded from this pleasant meeting! Standing: Ivy Yelland, Edith Purse, May Watts, Betty Evely, Mrs Brock, Carrie Marsden, Mrs S. Wilkinson. Sitting: May Marles, Harriet Hopkins, Ella Evans, Laura Friend.

"Dare Married Men express their opinions? – a 100% Human Drama!" screamed the newspaper headlines. In fact the packed courtroom was amused by stories of matrimonial bliss. It was the first Okehampton Flitch Trial, held in the market hall on 30 November 1931, with the proceeds being donated to charity. The judge was J. J. Newcombe, Town Clerk of Okehampton, an austere figure in Santa Claus robe and a full-bottomed wig, and lively humour between judge, counsel and witnesses kept the crowd amused for over three hours. The jury consisted of seven bachelors and six spinsters and they awarded the Flitch to Mr and Mrs Robert Middleton, a ham to Mr and Mrs William Middleton and a leg of mutton to Mr and Mrs Chowings, the only three contestants. Amongst those pictured are S. J. (Sam) Rich, G. Blatchford, solicitor Wilfred Fullwood, G. U. Fulford Bray, Banker White and two of the contestants.

It was Evensong at the Okehampton Castle Chapel in 1911 and the First Troop Okehampton Boy Scouts Bugle and Drum Bands, with choir, perform with Sydney Simmons as their guest of honour. We thought we would have great difficulty putting names to faces in this old photograph but former long-serving scout leader Victor Lenton came to our rescue, identifying all but one. Baden Powell had started the Boy Scout movement in 1908 and the Okehampton troop was thought to be one of the first in the country when it was formed in the same year. Many of the scouts featured in the photograph went on to become familiar names in the business life of Okehampton. The Bugle and Drum Band was also a welcome addition in the town. Having

already given Simmons Park, Sydney Simmons went on to purchase Okehampton Castle, which he donated to the town on 21 May 1917. He is the town's greatest benefactor, giving and contributing so many things which still bear his name. Back row: Bill Howse, Kirby Tippett, Bert Horn, B. Horsham. Middle row: D. Hodge, George Hutchings, George Richards, W. Harris, (?), Carol Oliver (standard bearer), Horace Weaver, W. Horne, Ted Webb, J. Lias, Harvey Hopkins. Front row: Ted Lias, Ernest Baker, Langley Powlesland (assistant scoutmaster), Rev D. Smidt, Sydney Simmons, Rev Stanley Carden MA (vicar and scoutmaster), Sid Coombe (bandmaster), Gus Libby, Austin Watkins. Sitting: Charlie Hodge, Cecil Landick.

The Motor Cycle Club of Okehampton were photographed in 1922 in this well-supported annual event – with not a crash helmet in sight. It was the motor cycle rally to Land's End and back, held on Good Friday and starting at 6.30 a.m. The photograph also provides an intriguing view of the south side of Fore Street, as it was in the 1920s. Just to the right of the archway was the Central Hotel, described on its fascia as "Family and Commercial Hotel", then comes Marks, Pastry Cooks and Confectioners, and the drapers, Drew & Lawson, all very respectable businesses of the time. Amongst the riders were Messrs Luxton, Downs, Newman, Horne, Backway, Yeo, Woods, Hoskins, Hawkins, Spencer, C. Bray and H. Bray, Tomlinson and J. Spencer. As the round trip would take about 12 hours or so, at 7 p.m. the riders would begin to roar in. It is interesting to note that the sober-suited members of the business community were not dressed like the motor cycle riders of today.

The Girls' Life Brigade (GLB) entered into the spirit of things with this prize-winning tableau in the 1958 Okehampton carnival. The entry was based on the popular song "The Story of our Lives". Bronwyn Symons played the storytelling grandmother, with Carol Jewell as grandfather. The grandchildren were played by Margaret Brock, Elizabeth Passmore and Jennifer Northam. Rosemary Dawkins was the groom and Beryl Eveleigh the bride, whilst Pat Goodanew, Jennifer Allin, Eileen Angel and Sally Connor completed this delightful tableau.

The successful fashion shows of the 1960s and 1970s were a regular feature of Okehampton business and social life. Hilda Twining of the Little Cherub, Marilyn Wheaton of the Yorkshire Stores and Joan Yeo organised their own shows with consummate professionalism, with charity being the beneficiary. Joan sponsored this show at the White Hart Hotel on 12 September 1962, with the lovely ladies casting aside their inhibitions to model lingerie and underwear. Joan tells us that many tradespeople in the town were most helpful in providing items to assist and perhaps ensure a front seat! The result of another successful evening was a substantial donation to the swimming pool. One of the models damaged her foot on the morning of the show and Joan was looking for a replacement. A holidaymaker, on the top left, called in at Joan's Salon for a shampoo and set; she was the right size, an experienced model and the rest is history. Back row: A holiday-maker, Marcia Stanbury, Mrs Windeatt, Brenda Maddaford, Florence Hughes, Heather Twining. Front row: Dilys Jordan, Jacky Wonnacott, (?), Val Uren, Joan Evans, Diane Pedrick, Jennifer Bassett.

This is in the nature of a valedictory photograph of the old board trustees of the Okehampton War Memorial Hospital. It was taken to mark the disappearance of the old structure and its absorption into the National Health scheme in 1948. It is interesting to note that in the previous year the daily average cost per patient was £1.2s.5d (£1.12), with the average cost per case being £12.16s.7d (£12.83). It is a tribute to these trustees and many other supporters and voluntary

helpers from the town and district that the hospital achieved such excellent results. It fulfilled, and continues so to do, a very pressing need and has proved of untold value to many people. Consulting physicians and surgeons, radiologists, dental surgeons and dentists freely gave their time. There were individual annual donations, collections from churches and public houses and house to house collections. There was also the "Egg Week". Under the guidance of the chairman, the worthy ladies of the Linen League regularly darned all the linen and annually donated sheets, quilts and pillowcases – a marvellous effort.

Back row: R. W. Kew, W. J. Avery, Dr E. D. Allen-Price, Mrs H. C. Brown, Mr W. C. Cowling, Ref F. E. Compton, Mr Bailey. Seated: C. E. W. (Clem) White (Secretary), Mrs V. Parsons, Mr W. H. Passmore, Matron H. M. Rosevear, Dr D. J. L. Routh, Miss M. M. Geen JP, Mr G. H. Gratton.

Matron Talbot was a popular figure at Okehampton Castle Hospital for many years. Her retirement presentation in 1961 was made by Dr Dan Twining accompanied by three other respected and long serving doctors, Shields, Jowett and Jones. Left to right: Sister Barron, Mr Talbot (administrator), Dr Shields, Dr Jowett, Dr Jones, Matron Talbot, Nurse Penhallurick, Dr Twining, Nurse Mason, Nurse Williams, Nurse Evans, Charge Nurse Sandy Powell, Nurse Johns, Nurse Waiters, Nurse Wooldridge, Nurse Gay.

In 1977 it was Dr Dan Twining's turn to retire, the presentation being made by hospital administrator Dennis Sampson. Mrs Twining is in the middle. The large gathering was a testament to the appreciation for many years of service devoted to his patients and the people of Okehampton and District.

The vast crowd gathered in Fore Street for the Coronation of King George V and Queen Mary celebrated in style. It was an opportunity for photographers to record those scenes of 22 July 1911 for posterity. One produced a series of postcards to commemorate the event, which comprised a full and varied programme. We have selected just two in the series. No 12 (above) is outside the Town Hall at 11.30 a.m. where the address from the borough to the King is about to be read by the Town Clerk, Mr J. J. Newcombe. John Cornish, the Mayor, is on the platform with Mrs Cornish and the two macebearers.

No 2 in the series (below) gives an indication of the size of the crowd as 'B' Company of the 6th Devon Territorial Regiment are about to fire "The Salute". A part of the festivities was a tea for girls and boys in Simmons Park given by Mr and Mrs Sydney Simmons, although, perhaps as a sign of the times, the girls were provided with their tea at 3.30 p.m and the boys at 4.30 p.m.

One of the most memorable events in Okehampton during the century was the Coronation of Her Majesty Queen Elizabeth II in 1953. The civic dignitaries are assembled outside the Town Hall, ready to make their way to the bottom of the Arcade for the 10.15 a.m. march past. Dr Jones, besides serving as an Alderman and Councillor for many years, was a popular general practitioner in the town. J. J. Newcombe was Town Clerk for over half a century and Alan Brunskill, the Borough Engineer and Surveyor, spent nearly his entire professional career in Okehampton. Left to right: J. J. Newcombe (Town Clerk), Bill Brock, Alderman Passmore (hidden), Jimmy Johns (macebearer), Borough Treasurer, Bill Cornish, G. U. Fulford, Dr C. G. Jones (Mayor), R. Alan Brunskill (Borough Surveyor), Reg Kennard, Harry Smith (macebearer), Mr Parsons (special constable), Reg Ellis (special constable), Ern Marles (special constable).

The day started at 7.40 a.m. with a peal on the parish church bells. This was followed by a floral dance in Fore Street at 8 a.m., which seemed to be attended by every local child, with adults joining in. The celebrations continued throughout the day, with a public tea between 4 p.m. and 6 p.m. also in Fore Street, followed by dancing there at 9.15 p.m. and culminating in the lighting of bonfires at 10 p.m. The Coronation was celebrated through a week to remember, commencing on Sunday 31 May and finishing on Saturday 6 June.

A feature of the Okehampton Ladies' Putting season was their annual fixture against the Town Council, always providing a close contest and plenty of good humour. This 1972 group is packed with outstanding personalities whose contribution to the town and community can never be measured but is, nevertheless, appreciated. Pictured left to right are: Peter Woodgate, Reg Horn, Nell Webb, Kay Giddy, Rose Stinchcombe, Doris Healey, Miss Tippett, Gladys Hayhurst, (?), Jimmy Crocker, Walter Passmore, Bill Letchford, Mrs Coombe, Polly White, Ron Taylor, Beatrice Fullwood, Joan Pauley, Margaret Weaver, Jeffe Cunliffe, Kay Judge, Susie Brock, Clem White, Ellen Hoare and Terry Bennett.

The Okehampton and District British Legion started the annual "Cheerio Day" in 1947. It was a day packed with events, starting early morning with the Gay Gordons and Floral Dance, right through to the afternoon with children's and adults' sports and sideshows, culminating in a gala dance at the Market Hall, admission 2s.6d (12p). The "Children's Pet Corner" was organised by a great character, farmer and dealer R. C. (Ginger) Hawkins, pictured right with Bob Squires (middle) and Raymond Maddaford (left). Hilary Bird and Tony Lowe are the intrepid riders and Jennifer Lowe is the cute little character to the right of Raymond. "Cheerio Days" were a great success, drawing huge crowds to the Pleasure Grounds, and it was a great pity when they ceased.

(Opposite, top) The Okehampton Male Voice Choir enhanced their reputation in post-war Okehampton by singing carols in Fore Street as Christmas 1947 approached. Including some great characters amongst those pictured are: Norman Moore, Ben Grainger, Norman Bickle (Conductor), Les Jeffery, Jim Richardson, "Shiner" Hoare, Freddie Hayhurst, Ralph Leach and Tom Evans. Freddie Hayhurst, besides being a director of John Cornish Ltd, was a councillor for many years, as well as serving a term as mayor of Okehampton.

The picture below is of the annual Combined Girls' Life Brigade and Boys' Brigade Christmas Party, 1957, in the Congregational Church Hall, North Street (now Okehampton Library).The Brigades had a dedicated band of helpers, most of whom are included in this photograph, which should revive happy memories. The compère was the jovial Trefor Lloyd Williams, who was seldom without a smile on his face, whether at work with SWEB or at play! Back row: Michael Evans, Alan Cox, Kenneth Gaywood, Alistair Macbeth, Walter Passmore, Michael Thwaites, Trefor Williams, Miss Glanfield. Fourth row: Alan Furze, Paddy Collacott, Julia Ball, Ann Shaw, Betty Dawe, Dilys Jordan, Hilary Bird, Janet Brewer, David Eveleigh, Diana Worden. Third row: Ron Hayhurst, Mrs Taylor, Rev Taylor, Cecily Medland, Mrs Macbeth, Mrs Marsden, Mrs Grace Brewer, Elizabeth Brooks, Mavis Hosgood, Margaret Angel, Pat Dawkins. Second row: Kathleen Medland, Gillian Hosgood, Thelma Dustan, Margaret Barkwill, Anita Luxton, Sheila Kelly, Bob Letchford, Trixie Spencer, Mrs Daisy Passmore, Miss Joan Pauley. Front row: Graham Hosgood, Ken Williams, Mary Westlake, Billy Lodge, Cynthia Walters, Jennifer Hosgood, Terry Acton.

The Girls' Life Brigade were a busy lot, always involved in something for their experience in life or for the good of others. They did, however, record many of their activities for the camera and, in 1954, they posed for this group photograph at the old Primary School in North Street. Back row: (?), Elizabeth Brooks, Margaret Angel, Paddy Collacott, Diane Worden, Cathy Medland, Joan Pauley, Gillian Hosgood, Eileen Angel, Bronwyn Lobb, Pat Goodanew, Elizabeth Lake, Bronwyn Symons, Rosemary Dawkins. Middle row: Pauline Jewell, Mary Connor, Janet Brewer, Mavis Hosgood, (?), Sheila Crook, Beryl Evely, Judith Powell, Jenny Allin, Christine Acton, Pat Dawkins (Standard Bearer). Front row: (?), Sally Connor, Cecily Medland, Anita Luxton, Margaret Barkwill, Sally Weeks, Louise Jewell, Linda Hosgood, Elizabeth Passmore, Carol Hubber, Ann Mortimore.

There was great rejoicing in Okehampton in 1890 when the original Swimming Bath, measuring 100 feet by 30 feet, was opened at Western Park, popularly known as the Old Park, opposite the Castle. There was no treatment for the bathing water, as it was kept fresh (and cold) by the maintenance of a constant flow of water from the nearby West Okement river. It was operated for many years by the Okehampton Bathing Association Ltd; it gave many generations of families their first opportunity to swim and local schools made every effort to use it. Prior to 1939, it was also the scene of many swimming events and galas.These photographs of a gala at the beginning of the century are so indicative of the times – the weather was hot but, nevertheless, hats must be worn and as for those voluminous dresses …!

One of the most dynamic organisations in the town was the Okehampton and District Swimming Pool Association (ODSPA). Recognising the need to have a new swimming pool, it was formed in 1962 and within five years had raised the necessary money (£18,500). It was open air at the time but it represented a great improvement on the Victorian "Bath". Soon, another £1,500 was raised to heat the pool and then further monies were raised to enclose it. This was later formally handed over to the Okehampton Town Council, who appointed a Trust Committee to administer it. It is now run by the West Devon Borough Council. It was originally opened by the Mayor of Okehampton, Mr. W. J. Passmore, on 12 August 1967 and its plaque reads "Commemorating the achievements of ODSPA who, by their endeavours, made the provision of this swimming pool possible". It is a fitting tribute to the men and women who gave so much time and hard work to bring this project to fruition. A swimming pool is an expensive item and ODSPA held many events to raise money, including, in 1976, a sponsored walk by children around Simmons Park. Pictured here is hardworking ODSPA member and popular mayor Jeffe Cunliffe with a bevy of excited children outside the Simmons Park pavilion. A provision of the selected circuit was that the children had to be in sight of the mayor at all times – safety first! Needless to say, with parents, aunts, uncles and grandparents all contributing, a substantial amount was raised and put to good use.

The Headquarters of the old "B" Division of the Devon Constabulary was at the George Street Police Station. There was a large membership from the specials and the Hatherleigh Sub Division, under the motivation of the Section Sergeant Brian Pinney, enjoyed exceptional support. This picture shows the final "get together" at Easter 1965 of the Hatherleigh Section Special Constabulary. The following August, Brian was moved to Okehampton when the station closed and the specials were divided between Holsworthy, North Tawton, Okehampton and Torrington. Brian Pinney was later awarded the MBE. We were only able to identify the officers in the front row of this photograph and they are (left to right): S/Sgt. Harold Cork, S/Sgt. Bert Trenaman, S/Sgt. Jack Edwards, Sgt. Brian Pinney, S/lnsp. George Weeks, S/Sub. Insp. Clarrie Westaway, S/Sgt. Dick Pearce, S/Sgt. Bill Moast, S/Sgt. Jack Adams.

Throughout the years, the church choir has enjoyed a fine reputation and we have selected this group of 1974 as being representative of this. It includes a number of long-standing stalwarts. Back row: Jim Hannaford, Max Turner, Frank Cloke, Mr Sarah, Vic Lancaster, Lionel Kent. Third row: Paul Church, Stella Hudson, Christine Cann, Esme Hannaford, Christine Bond, Geoff Wooldridge. Second row: Martin Maddaford, Tony Patrick, Graham Church, Michael Ware, Christopher Kennard, Mark Curtis, John Kent. Front row: Lyn Weaver, Rev Kingsley Williams, Ref A. J. Radford, Rev Douglas, Ian Cann.

Between 1939 and 1945 the church bells remained silent, although prepared for ringing in the event of an invasion! They are an integral part of church life and the returning servicemen joined with the pre-war bellringers to form a new team. George Gale, the captain, rang the tenor, whilst his deputy, Bert Yeo, was an expert at the treble and also called the changes. This All Saints Parish Church bellringers' outing was in August 1946. The first port of call was Dartmouth, whilst the next church was a small one in South Devon, where George Gale had skilfully arranged the timetable so that, as soon as they finished ringing, it would coincide with the opening of the public house immediately opposite. Back row: Sid Caseley, Bert Yeo (Vice Captain), Sam Hucker, Tom Heale, Tom Brock, Sid Voysey. Front row: Fred Pope, Billy Isaac, Jimmy Johnson, George Gale (Captain), Sid Horn, Jack Hooper.

The custom of Beating the Bounds, sometimes called Spurling Day, continues to this very day and consists of perambulating the bounds of the old borough. It was a tradition to throw quantities of apples, nuts, etc, in "miry" places as they proceeded and the boys would scramble for them. We suppose, in this time of equal opportunities, that girls would now participate? In this pre-war photograph, amongst the horsemen are Ginger Hawkins, Skinner Hoare, Ken Stevens and Bert Pellow, whilst on foot Ern Kelly, Stan Trant, Bob Furze, Ernest Bassett, Lucy Hodge, Pearl Steer, Mona Cockwill, Mrs Northam, Mrs Piper and Mrs Chowings are instantly recognisable.

Part of the fun of Beating the Bounds are the stops for refreshments and the chance to rest weary limbs. The year is 1960 and the willing helpers, including some expert 'moormen', are getting ready for the walk at Newtake. Left to right: Bill Voaden, Reg Ward, young Robert Cunliffe, Tommy Hodge, Mrs Bevan, Sam Wooldridge, Mrs Voysey, Arthur Painter, George Whieldon, Mrs Piper, Ginger Hawkins, Mrs Bert Hawkins, Mrs Harris and Sister Hawkins.

(Opposite, top) Okehampton has had many celebrated bands over the years, such as the Borough, Town Military, Territorial Army Bugle, Volunteer Corps, Salvation Army, Boys' Brigade and String and Wind Orchestras and more besides. There were also the "Thirsty Eight", named for obvious reasons, and the Okehampton Mandolin Band. However, it is the Okehampton Excelsior Band, of more recent years, which we have decided to feature as a tribute to the work and enthusiasm of their present long-serving musical director, Reg Beardon. This band probably owes its origins to bandmaster Barber Coombes, who initially formed a band under his own name in 1856 which was reformed and renamed the Excelsior Band in 1912. Reg had started under bandmaster Ogden with the old Borough Band at the tender age of nine. It was when he started with SWEB in 1949, as an Electrical Apprentice to R. T. (Bob) Gale, who was the son of Jimmy Gale of the Excelsior, that he changed his allegiance. Bob "persuaded" Reg that it would be in his best interests to transfer to the Excelsior! He was subsequently appointed musical director of the band in 1971 at a time of great change, as many of the senior members were, or had, retired, but he is quick to praise the help of the ones who stayed. Remembering his own formative years, he started a junior section and we have selected two photographs from many which illustrate his great successes over the years. Back row: Robert Kelly, Jacob Mooney, Adam Mooney. Middle row: Nicky Brazier, David Allin, Trudy Short, Graham Mitchell, Valerie Packer, Jill Kelly, Gary Stevens, Teresa Warren, Nicky Warren, Sandra Vaugan, Rebecca Mooney, Richard Baker, Andrew Gilbert, Philip Martin, Andrew Packer. Front row: Paul Baker, Angie Warren, Jayne Hawkings, Jo Brazier, Louise Hawkings, Reg Beardon, Tracey Middleton, Karen Milton, Angie McCullock, Andrew Martin.

(Opposite, bottom) We make no apologies for using this recent 1997 photograph, following a triumphant visit to Wesseling in Germany. The Excelsior had been selected to represent the West Devon District in an international concert, where they played with bands from seven other European countries. A crowning glory was that Reg was nominated to conduct the finale of all

the massed bands in playing "Land of Hope and Glory" – the ultimate honour – Reg, the man with the grand band. Back row: Paul Chammings, Robert Peerless, Rebecca Hood, Mike Isaac, Roger Law, Jim Crook, Martin Clear. Middle row: Imogen Reed, Louise Beardon, Julie Hood, Jo Ware, Alison King, Richard Beardon, Ian Marvin, Liz Pendleton, Barrie Pillivant. Front row: George Brazier, Julie King, Valerie Isaac, Jayne Pillivant, Reg Beardon, Dean Beardon, Emma Gillard, David Allin, Timothy Hood, Des Law.

Starting in 1920, the DMT (Devon Motor Transport) spread its network of carrier and passenger service throughout Devon. In fact, DMT became so popular that it was often referred to as "Does Most Things". The company came into being at a time when the possibilities of road transport were clearly foreseen. It was started through the enterprise of an ex-serviceman and from the commencement he gave preference to the employment of ex-servicemen. The scheme was very successful and he built on this with selected apprentices from the local schools. The company expanded by buying existing companies and opening routes through Devon and Cornwall. DMT quickly integrated into the Okehampton community and would participate in any event, with the annual carnival being a particular favourite, an opportunity to put their engineering skills to good use. This entry for the 1926 carnival advertised their Okehampton to Lands End service, while the vehicle was described as the "Pride of the Midget Fleet". Amongst the staff are Inspector Trollope, Dick Northcott, Percy Knight, Sparky Lang, Percy Mogridge, Tim Shobbrook and "Old Man" Lovell.

DMT formed a Sports and Social Club and, with its large workforce, could field good sides. The football team played in the West Devon League and, as the Okehampton Ivyleaves were in the same division, there were some local derbies to enjoy. In the summer, many of the footballers played cricket for the DMT representative side and they chose Simmons Park for this evocative picture prior to a match against Okehampton Cricket Club in 1926. Back row: H. Innes, J. Knight, S. Wreford, E. V. Schuster, R. S. Lang (Treasurer), A. Saunders, V. Innes (Assistant Secretary). Front row: C. Rich, S. J. Easterbrook (Captain), S. R. Northcott, G. R. Lang (Secretary), L. Bolitho. In 1930, this enterprise, with its 200 or so staff based at West Street, where Jacobs Pool now stands, was itself taken over and the Okehampton operation came to an end.

The staff of Day's, like DMT, enjoyed carnivals and would also participate in any other event where they could exploit their creative skills. This beautifully lit and attractive window display was for the firm to celebrate the Silver Jubilee of King George V on 6 May 1935. The King had, as the Prince of Wales, garaged his car at Day's some 27 years earlier. This showroom was just past West Bridge and was demolished in 1956.

The Okehampton sports week was a popular annual event and the cricket knock-out was always keenly fought. The 1974 final was between the Buffs and the Okehampton branch of the South Western Electricity Board, who ran out winners in a sporting and close clash. The cricketers in this photograph are (left to right): Roy Curtis, Raymond Piper, Les Gliddon, Mike Simmons, Bob Chapman, Chris Ball, Kenny Galvin, John King, Brian Ainsley, Brian Ellis, Roy Wilton (Umpire), Mike Palmer, Mike Wreford, Charlie Curtis, John Wright, Terry Bevan, Sid Sanders, Jim Bulley, Graham Partridge, Trevor Drew, Colin Letchford, Phil Hannaford, Bob Symons, Rod Crabtree (Umpire).

One of the great traditions of the Simmons Bowling Club is that each year the Mayor of Okehampton opens the season by bowling the first wood. In 1977, without a raincoat in sight, it was the turn of Mayor Jeffe Cunliffe and Mayoress Peggy to perform the ceremony. Amongst the members are Mesdames May, Hubber, Adams, Luxton and Mills, Messrs Bob Furse, Roy Lobb, Tregaskis, Roberts, C. Pedrick, R. Moore, S. Vernon, Don England and Percy Adams. The inception of this fine bowling club owed much to Sydney Simmons, who donated £800 towards this and the tennis courts in 1922. When the Simmons Bowling Club was formed, he was deservedly appointed its President and life patron – another honour for this great man.

Largely non-political, the teams of the Okehampton Labour Club and Okehampton Liberal Club in the Okehampton and District Billiard League in 1953 proudly display their trophies. Sadly these two social clubs are no more, but the league continues as a snooker league, giving much pleasure to the players in the town and villages in the dark winter evenings, with their comradeship. Ron (Digger) Stoneman, Eric Chowings, Dave Travers, Ron Cox, Gerald Uren, Eric "Champ" Medland, George Maddaford, Derek Lee, Brian Weaver, Raymond Frost and Colin "Wally" Travers are shown in this picture.